6/07

The Biography of Cotton

Carrie Gleason

 Crabtree Publishing Company
www.crabtreebooks.com

Crabtree Publishing Company
www.crabtreebooks.com

For my mom, Sandy

Coordinating editor: Ellen Rodger
Editors: Rachel Eagen, Adrianna Morganelli, L. Michelle Nielsen
Production coordinator: Rosie Gowsell
Production assistance: Samara Parent
Art director: Rob MacGregor
Photo research: Allison Napier

Photo Credits:
Musee des Beaux-Arts, Pau, France, Giraudon/Bridgeman Art Library: p. 20 (bottom); Victoria & Albert Museum, London, UK/Bridgeman Art Library: p. 15 (top); New-York Historical Society, New York, USA/Bridgeman Art Library: p. 20 (top); Private Collection/Bridgeman Art Library: p. 4 (bottom left), p. 16, p. 17 (top); Private Collection, Index/Bridgeman Art Library: p. 14 (top); Royal Asiatic Society, London, UK/Bridgeman Art Library: p. 5 (top); Smithsonian Institution, Washington DC, USA/Bridgeman Art Library: p. 17 (bottom); Pallava Bagla/Corbis: p. 7 (bottom); Roger Ball/Corbis: p. 10 (bottom), p. 11 (top); Bettmann/Corbis: p. 18, p. 21 (bottom), p. 23, p. 26 (both), p. 29 (bottom); Lowell Georgia/Corbis: p. 11 (bottom); Jeremy Horner/Corbis: p. 1; Craig Lovell/Corbis: p. 13 (bottom); Michael Nicholson/Corbis: p. 15 (top); Richard T. Nowitz/Corbis: p. 29 (top); Gianni Dagli Orti/Corbis: p. 12 (bottom); Owaki-Kulla/Corbis: p. 3; Neil Rabinowitz/Corbis: p. 21 (top); Richard Hamilton Smith/Corbis: p. 9 (bottom), p. 10 (top); Stapleton Collection/Corbis: p. 13 (top); Anatoliy Babiychuck/istock International: p. 5 (bottom); James E. Hernandaz/istock International: p. 8 (top); Ansley Johnson/istock International: p. 8 (bottom); Julie de Leseleuc/istock International: p. 4 (bottom right), p. 9 (top); Michel Mory/istock International: p. 8 (middle); Dan Gair Photographic/maXximages.com: cover; North Wind Picture Archives: p. 12 (top), p. 14 (bottom), p. 19 (both), p. 22, p. 24, p. 25, p. 27; Gerd Ludwig/Visum/Panos Pictures: p. 7 (top); Fernando Moleres/Panos Pictures: p. 30; Karen Robinson/Panos Pictures: p. 31; Norm Thomas/Photo Researchers, Inc.: p. 28; USDA/Photo Researchers, Inc.: p. 9 (middle); Other images from stock cd.

Cartography: Jim Chernishenko: p. 6

Cover: In India, most of the cotton crop is still picked by hand. India is a top producer of cotton.

Title page: A cloth merchant in a bazaar stall pulls out a bolt of cotton fabric to show his customers. Cotton fabric is sold this way in the cities and towns of India and Pakistan.

Contents page: Rows of cotton plants with bolls ready for picking.

Crabtree Publishing Company

www.crabtreebooks.com   1-800-387-7650

Cataloging-in-Publication Data

Gleason, Carrie, 1973-
  The biography of cotton / written by Carrie Gleason.
    p. cm. -- (How did that get here?)
  Includes index.
  ISBN-13: 978-0-7787-2480-3 (rlb)
  ISBN-10: 0-7787-2480-8 (rlb)
  ISBN-13: 978-0-7787-2516-9 (pb)
  ISBN-10: 0-7787-2516-2 (pb)
  1. Cotton--Juvenile literature. I. Title. II. Series.
TS1542.G64 2005
677'.21--dc22   2005023002
                                                       LC

**Published in
the United States**
PMB 16A
350 Fifth Ave.
Suite 3308
New York, NY
10118

**Published
in Canada**
616 Welland Ave.
St. Catharines
Ontario, Canada
L2M 5V6

**Published in the
United Kingdom**
73 Lime Walk
Headington
Oxford
OX3 7AD
United Kingdom

**Published
in Australia**
386 Mt. Alexander Rd.
Ascot Vale (Melbourne)
VIC 3032

Contents

What is Cotton?

Much of the clothing we wear is made from cotton. Cotton is also used to make bed sheets and other home furnishings as well as cotton balls and cotton swabs. Cotton is a natural fiber that grows on the cotton plant. Fibers are long and short, thin threads. There are many types of natural fibers that are made into cloth, such as linen, which comes from the flax plant, and wool, from sheep's fleece. Of all the different types of natural fibers, cotton is the most widely used today.

Why Cotton?

Cotton is a commodity. Commodities are goods that are traded and sold. Until the early 1800s, cotton goods were not widely available, except in the areas where the plants were grown. Today, cotton is shipped and **processed** around the world. People demand cotton because of the **quality** products it is made into. Clothing made from cotton absorbs moisture and is easily dyed different colors. Cotton clothing is also lightweight, cool to wear, and affordable.

▲ *The cotton boll, or seedpod.*

(left) Cotton became a major crop in the southern United States in the early 1800s when slaves were brought to work on cotton plantations.

Rags to Riches

During a period of history known as the **Industrial Revolution**, some mill owners became very wealthy turning cotton fibers into yarn and thread. Some home-based craftspeople, who feared machines were taking over the ancient skill of making cloth, vandalized, or destroyed, mills and the homes of mill owners. In the United States, by the 1800s, both farming areas and many cities were dependent on the harvesting of cotton and manufacturing of cloth. The history of cotton is the story of the people who worked to make cotton cheap and widely available, from the inventors of the Industrial Revolution, to the slaves of the American South, and the first young women mill workers of the North.

▸ *The cotton plant with flowers and bolls. Cotton bolls produce a fiber that is made into cloth for clothing and other fabrics.*

Jeans are made from a cotton cloth called denim. Jeans were first made in the American West by Levi Strauss in 1873, and were sold as workpants for cowboys.

Cotton Lands

Cotton plants grow in the subtropics, or warm areas of the world just north and south of tropical regions. Cotton plants need a lot of water when they are young. As they grow, the plants also need a lot of sunlight.

The First Cotton Plants

Scientists who study plants, called botanists, believe that cotton plants first grew about seven million years ago. Different species, or types, of cotton plants grew wild in different areas. Over millions of years, the seeds of the plants, covered in a tough skin called a boll or pod, traveled from their place of origin on ocean currents and took root far from home. The traveling seeds **crossbred** with native cotton plants to produce new species.

Types of Plants

There are four main types of cotton plants. Two of these, *G. arboreum* (Asiatic cotton) and *G. herbaceum* (Arabian cotton or Levant cotton), are considered Old World plants, which means they emerged in Asia, Europe, or Africa. The other two main species, *G. barbandense* (Sea Island or American Pima) and *G. hirsutum*, also called upland cotton, are from the **New World**.

The United States is the biggest exporter of cotton in the world. China is the largest producer of cotton. In the United States, cotton is grown mostly in the southern states of Texas, Georgia, Mississippi, Arkansas, North Carolina, and Louisiana.

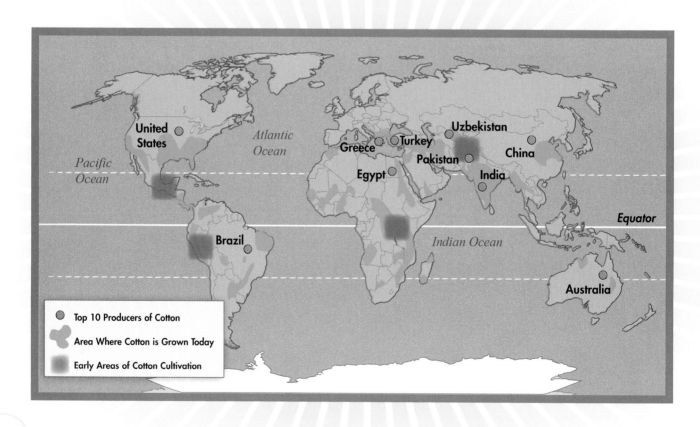

The Case of the Missing Water

Cotton is often grown in warm areas of the world that receive little rainfall. Without rain, farmers must **irrigate** crops so they get enough water to grow. In Uzbekistan and Kazakhstan, in Central Asia, water to irrigate cotton is taken from rivers that feed the Aral Sea. The Aral Sea is a large salt lake that lies between the two countries. So much water has been diverted from it that its water level is dangerously low. The local fishing industry has been wiped out because of the low water level and the high level of salt in the water. Pesticides, or chemicals sprayed on crops to keep harmful pests away, also polluted the water and soil. With so much of the lake's bed exposed and contaminated, windstorms kick up poisonous dust and make the people living in the area sick.

(above) Cotton became a major crop in Central Asia in the 1960s. So much water was used to grow cotton that the Aral Sea shrunk in size, leaving fishing boats stuck on dry land.

The Textile Industry

Fibers from the cotton plant are called raw cotton. Raw cotton is manufactured, or made into textiles. Textiles are then made into clothing and other goods. Textile manufacturing is a huge industry. In some countries where cotton is grown, all raw cotton is used to support an indigenous, or native, textile industry. India is the third-largest producer of cotton, but it exports, or sells to other countries, very little of its raw cotton. India's textile industry is so large that it has to import, or buy in, raw cotton from other countries.

(left) About 15 million people in India work in the textile industry.

From Fiber to Fabric

Cotton fibers are twisted together to create thread or yarn, from which textiles are woven or knit. Cotton fibers vary in length and color. The length of the cotton fiber is important in manufacturing. Different types of cotton plants produce different lengths of fibers. Short cotton fibers easily break apart and make coarser fabric. Inch-long, or medium-staple fibers from upland cotton, are the most commonly used today. Long fibers produce the strongest, softest fabrics.

Seeds and Plants

In North America, farmers plant cotton from seeds in spring. They use planting machines that drop seeds in rows. These rows are about four feet (one meter) apart. Cotton fields are kept clear of weeds while the plants grow. Weeds steal the **nutrients** from the soil that growing plants need. After about three months, flowers appear on the cotton plants. The flowers live for only three days. They die, fall off, and are replaced by small seedpods called bolls.

Cotton plants before bloom and in bloom. The yellow and red flowers fall off and are replaced by seedpods called bolls.

Cotton Bolls

It takes several months for cotton bolls to grow. During this time, moist cotton fibers form around the seeds. Inside each boll are about 30 seeds. In early fall, when the plants have grown into bushes about four feet (one meter) tall, the seeds ripen and the cotton bolls open up to reveal fluffy white cotton fibers. There are about 500,000 fibers inside a single cotton boll.

▲ A raw cotton boll.

Cotton Picking

When the seed bolls open up, the cotton is ready to be picked. In some countries, such as the United States and Australia, large mechanical harvesters, or machines, pick the cotton. There are two types of cotton harvesters. Strippers move over the cotton plants picking both the open and unopened cotton bolls. Pickers remove the cotton from the open bolls using a rotating spindle that moves over the sticky cotton fibers, and picks them up. In other countries, such as China, India, and Pakistan, cotton is harvested by hand. Handpicking cotton is a slow process that requires many laborers who work long hours in the hot sun.

(left) The fluffy white handful of cotton has been ginned and is ready for making into yarn at a textile mill.

Machines harvest cotton in Mississippi. Cotton is still harvested by hand in some countries.

Ginnery

Harvested cotton is usually taken to a factory called a ginnery. At a ginnery, the fibers are removed from the seeds by a machine called a cotton gin. The leaves, branches, and other field dirt are also removed. The fibers are cleaned and dried in a separate machine. They are then **pressed** into large bales weighing 500 lbs (227 kg) each. The bales are tied with steel bands and loaded onto ships to be sent to mills.

(above) Piles of cotton are processed by a cotton gin in a Mississippi field.

Textile Mills

At a textile mill, or factory, cotton fibers are twisted together to make yarn or thread. The first step at the mill is to open up the cotton bales and break up the compressed fibers. The next step is carding and combing. Carding untangles the twisted fibers and pulls them into a thin rope called a sliver. Combing removes the short fibers to make the sliver smoother. Sliver strands are twisted together to make a stronger strand called roving. The roving is drawn and twisted on machines to join the strands together in a process called spinning. The tighter the roving is wound, the stronger the thread or yarn. Finished yarn and thread are wound on large bobbins and are made into fabric.

(left) Bales of cotton in a warehouse.

Making Textiles

Cloth is made either by weaving or knitting. Weaving is done on machines called looms. Woven fabric is made by crossing one set of yarn, called the weft thread, over and under another set called the warp. Knit fabric is made on knitting machines. In knits, the yarn or thread is looped through itself row after row.

Finishing Cloth

Finishing is the final step in making cloth. Finishing includes a number of processes in which chemicals are added to cloth, and machines are used to change the cloth's texture. Chemicals make cotton cloth wrinkle-resistant or waterproof. Machines pre-stretch or preshrink fabric so that it will retain its shape when made into clothing. Finishing also involves bleaching cloth so that it can be dyed.

(right) Knitting or weaving machines turn cotton into fabric.

Large bobbins, or spools, of cotton yarn and thread are made at this factory in China.

Cotton in the Ancient World

Cotton plants were first cultivated, or grown as a crop, in about 3500 B.C. Civilizations, or peoples, living far apart from one another in India, South America, Africa, and Mexico harvested cotton and spun the fibers to make cloth. These ancient peoples, who had no contact with one another, developed similar tools for cleaning, spinning, and weaving cotton.

The Harappans

The ancient Harappan civilization developed in the Indus River Valley, in what is now Pakistan. The Harappans were probably the first people to cultivate Old World cotton. **Archaeologists** digging at sites found the remains of textiles that date back to about 2300 B.C. When the **Hindu** religion developed in the area, people on pilgrimages, or religious journeys, spread cotton seeds to the southern parts of India.

▲ *Fragments of cloth that are 5,000 years old have been found in a cave in Mexico.*

Early Cotton Trade

The earliest method for dyeing cotton cloth was developed by dyers in ancient India. Cotton cloth was soaked in animal urine or dung to make the dye stick to the fabric. This method of dying cloth remained an important trade secret of Indian cloth dyers for thousands of years. From India, cotton spread to Persia, Egypt, the Middle East, and eventually to Europe.

Andean Cultures

Around the same time that the Harappans in the Indus Valley started making cotton cloth, people in what is now Chile and Peru in South America also began to harvest cotton fibers. Cotton grew naturally in the Andes Mountains.

(above) Ancient peoples wove cotton on small hand looms like this one.

(left) In ancient Nubia and ancient Egypt, wealthy people wore cotton cloth traded from India. By 400 B.C., trade routes brought cotton across northern Africa to reach West Africa.

For the ancient Peruvians, weaving was a form of art as well as a way of making cloth. From South America, cotton spread to Central America and the Caribbean Islands. The cotton grew in many different colors, in shades that ranged from brown to light purple.

African Cotton

The cotton variety *G. herbaceum* first grew wild in sub-Saharan Africa, or areas of Africa south of the Equator. At first, the seeds of the plant were picked, boiled, and eaten for food. Cotton was first cultivated in Nubia, in what is now Ethiopia and the Sudan in eastern Africa. By 400 B.C., trade routes brought cotton across northern Africa to reach the West African kingdoms of Ghana, Mali, and Songhai.

Mayan and Aztec Cloth

In Central America, upland cotton grew wild and was cultivated in the Yucatan Peninsula, in what is now Mexico, by the Maya and Aztec peoples. The Aztec made cotton into strips called mantas using a loom. The mantas were so valuable that the last Aztec ruler, Montezuma, demanded them as a tribute, or a sign of respect, from the people in his **empire**.

Myth of the Loom

Women from many different cultures in South and Central America use a type of loom called a backstrap loom. The backstrap loom has been used for thousands of years. According to a Mayan legend, backstrap weaving was invented by Ixchel, the goddess of weaving and medicine.

The backstrap loom gets its name because one end of the loom is tied around the weaver's back, while the other end is tied around a tree.

Cotton Spreads

By the 600s A.D., overland trade routes from India to Venice, in what is now Italy, were controlled by **Arab** traders. These traders traveled across the deserts by camel caravans. They sold a fine cotton cloth called muslin and a colorful printed cotton cloth made in India called calico. Around 700 A.D., Arab traders brought cotton seeds to Spain from North Africa. Cotton grew well in southern Spain. Weaving centers were established in Spanish cities, such as Grenada, Cordova, and Seville. Much of the cotton was used to make a medieval cloth called fustian, which was a blend of cotton and wool or linen.

The East India Company

The English East India Company was formed in 1600. The company, which was made up of English merchants, was given permission by the English **crown** to control all trade with India. The East India Company brought large amounts of chintz and calico cotton to Europe using the sea route discovered earlier by Portuguese explorers. Chintz, a colorful cotton cloth, was popular among wealthy Europeans. Europeans did not know how to make the patterned cloth themselves because they could not make the dye stick to the cloth. The craze for Indian chintz was so great that in 1686 the French government made it illegal to import cotton cloth into France. French linen and silk manufacturers feared the cotton cloth from India would take over their business. After 1750, Europeans discovered the Indian secret of making dyed cloth and began to import raw cotton to make the cloth themselves.

(above) In 1498, Portuguese explorer Vasco da Gama sailed to India and returned to Europe with cargo that included cotton cloth.

(right) By 1784, American cotton was exported to England where it was seized because no one believed the massive shipment was grown in America.

America's Cotton

English settlers at Jamestown, Virginia, planted cotton among their crops after arriving to set up the first European colony in the United States in 1607. At first, the colonists harvested the cotton for their own use. By the late 1600s, farmers in Virginia and North and South Carolina were exporting cotton to other colonies. In 1784, American ships entered the port of Liverpool, England, carrying eight bales of cotton grown in the colonies. In England, authorities seized, or took possession of, the cargo because they believed that the colonists could not have grown so much cotton in the United States. By 1800, millions of pounds of cotton were being exported to England from the United States.

▸ *Calico cloth made in India was a fashionable fabric for women's gowns and curtains in Europe during the 1700s.*

(below) The W.G Taylor power loom was one machine that helped Europeans make calico cloth.

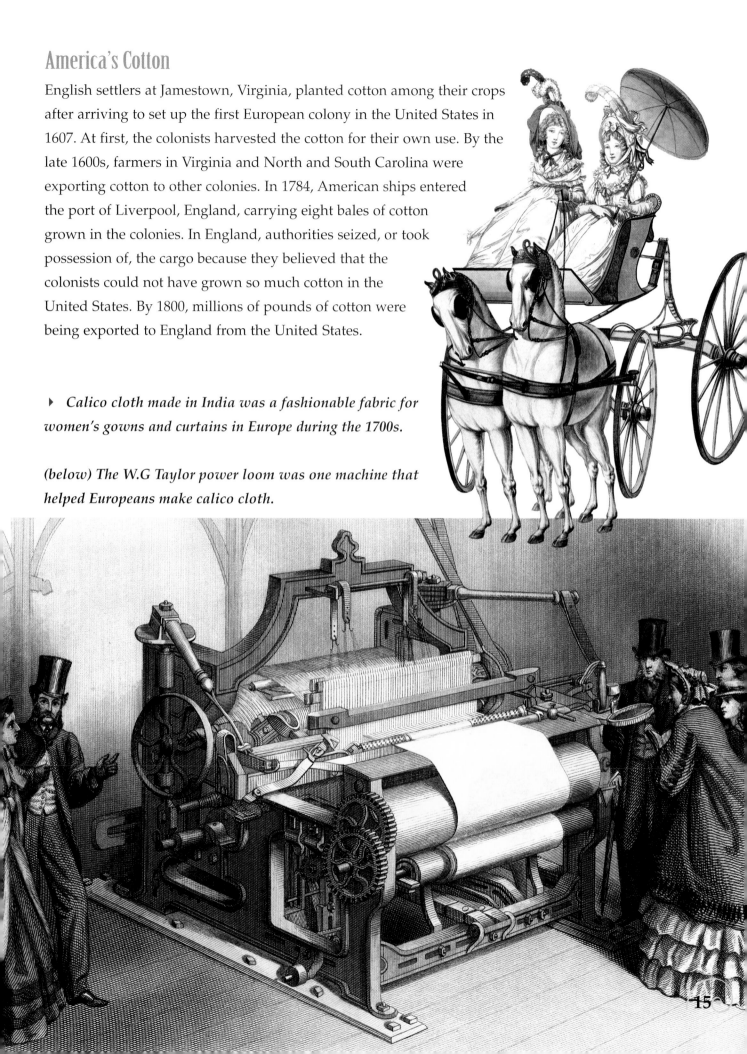

15

The early 1700s in England marked the beginning of a period of history called the Industrial Revolution. For thousands of years, all cloth had been made by hand in homes. Merchants supplied raw cotton for spinners and weavers to make the cloth and sold the finished goods. Home workers were paid by the amount of thread or cloth they produced. During the Industrial Revolution, machines were built that replaced the work previously done by hand.

Flying and Spinning

The first machine that sped up cotton cloth production was the flying **shuttle**. James Kay invented the flying shuttle in 1733 in England. The flying shuttle produced cloth faster than by hand. It sped up weaving so much that home-spinners could not keep up with the increased demand for thread.

Spinning Jenny

In 1764, the spinning jenny was invented by James Hargreaves to produce more thread faster. The spinning jenny was an improvement on the spinning wheel. It used eight spindles instead of just one, which were all controlled by just one wheel.

The Textile Revolution

Around the same time that inventions were being made in textile production, James Watt invented the steam engine. The steam engine was a new source of power. Before its invention, people relied on power from waterwheels to operate early machinery. Richard Arkwright had opened England's first textile mills in 1771, but they had to be built next to rivers. Then, in 1784, Edmund Cartwright invented the power loom. The power loom was a machine that could not be operated by hand. The inventions of the steam engine and the power loom lead to the building of the first cotton factories away from rivers, in English cities such as Manchester and Nottingham. People began to work in factories making cotton cloth instead of in their homes.

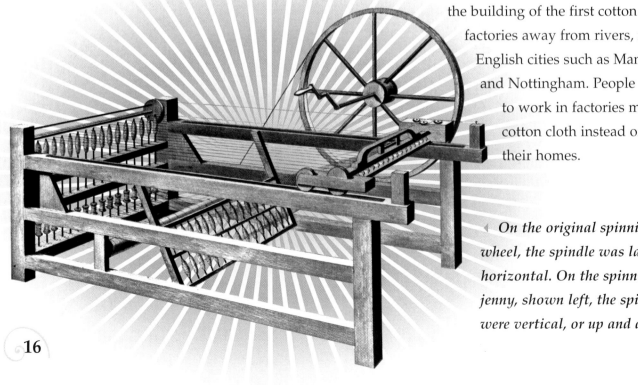

◄ On the original spinning wheel, the spindle was laid horizontal. On the spinning jenny, shown left, the spindles were vertical, or up and down.

Luddite Riots

Many home-based textile workers did not like that yarn and cloth were made in factories. A group of textile workers, called Luddites, feared that that the skill of workers was going to be replaced by machines that produced poor-quality textiles. The Luddites rioted and broke into textile factories at night to destroy the new machines. In 1812, the British government passed a law where people found guilty of breaking the machines could be sentenced to death.

To America

English mill owners tried to keep their machines a secret so that textiles could only be made in their mills. Laws were passed to keep mill workers from moving to other countries and spreading their knowledge of how the machines worked. In 1789, English mill worker Samuel Slater came to the United States dressed as a farm laborer. The United States had recently gained its independence from England. American leaders, such as President George Washington, were trying to establish manufacturing industries to lessen the country's dependence on the import of British manufactured goods. Slater opened the first cotton mill in the United States on the Blackstone River in Pawtucket, Rhode Island to spin yarn.

(below) The first cotton mill in the United States was established by Samuel Slater (1768-1835) at Pawtucket, Rhode Island.

The Cotton Gin

New inventions sped up the process for making cotton cloth and the demand for raw cotton rose. It took about one full day to pull free one pound of cotton fiber from the seeds. Farmers in the southern United States were limited in the amount of cotton they could produce because cotton was so difficult to harvest by hand. Most of the raw cotton needed to feed England's cotton factories was being supplied by India.

▼ *Eli Whitney's cotton gin was a revolution in cotton processing.*

Supply and Demand

Along the coasts of the southeastern United States, a variety of cotton called Sea Island cotton was grown and harvested. Sea Island cotton has long fibers that are easily removed from the seeds, but it only grows in coastal areas. In the interior, a type of cotton called upland cotton grew. Few planters grew upland cotton as a **cash crop** because the seeds were hard to extract from the sticky fibers. Other cash crops that grew in the South at this time were rice, which required a large amount of labor, and tobacco, which quickly drained the soil of its nutrients.

Whitney's Cotton Gin

Eli Whitney invented a machine called a cotton gin, or engine, in 1794. The cotton gin sped up the amount of cotton that could be pulled free of the seeds to 50 pounds (23 kilograms) by one worker in a single day. Whitney invented the machine after watching a slave do the work by hand. His gin worked by mimicking the movements of human hands picking seeds. To do the work of fingers pulling apart the fibers, Whitney built a rotating drum with little hooks on it. A wire filter held the seeds back while the fibers were pulled away. A brush rotating faster than the drum cleaned the lint off the hooks.

The Cotton Rush

Plantation, or large farm, owners immediately began to plant upland cotton after they learned of Eli Whitney's invention. Whitney entered into a partnership with the manager of Mulberry Grove, the plantation in Georgia where he had been staying. Together, the men decided they would build cotton gins and sell them for the price of one-third of plantation owners' cotton crops. Plantation owners found this price too steep. Their cotton was also ready to be harvested faster than the gins were built, so they made their own cotton gins, based on Whitney's design.

(right) Slaves use Whitney's cotton gin to process raw cotton.

Patents and Protection

Eli Whitney was slow in applying for a patent for his cotton gin. A patent is a government license that recognizes the inventor's machine and gives him or her the sole right to make, use, or sell the invention. Whitney was awarded a patent for his invention in 1794, but by that time, so many planters had built their own gins that Whitney could not protect his patent. In 1801, Whitney received a small **compensation** from the southern states for the invention that brought great wealth to the South.

Eli Whitney attended Yale College in Connecticut. Before that, he made his living as a blacksmith, a nail maker, and a maker of lady's hat pins.

King Cotton

Cotton **boomed** in the southern United States after the invention of the cotton gin. In an area that came to be known as the Cotton Belt, cotton was the main cash crop from the 1800s to the 1900s. The Cotton Belt included the southeastern states of North Carolina, South Carolina, Georgia, Alabama, and Mississippi, as well as western Tennessee, eastern Arkansas, Louisiana, eastern Texas, southern Oklahoma, and small areas of southeast Missouri, southwest Kentucky, northern Florida, and southeast Virginia. The climate of these areas allowed for cotton to thrive. Many farmers abandoned other crops, such as rice and tobacco, and plantations were established to grow only cotton. On cotton plantations, growing and harvesting cotton was done by slaves.

(above) Slaves who planted, cared for, and harvested the cotton crops lived on the plantations in poorly-built wooden shacks

(below) Major cities, such as New Orleans, Louisiana, became important centers of trade during the cotton boom. Exchange buildings were used to buy and sell cotton.

(above) Planters and their families lived in grand mansions, built with the profits of the cotton trade.

The Cotton Market

Agriculture was the main business of the South and its economy grew because of the demand for cotton. Cotton was shipped to the North and to England to be used in cotton mills. In 1790, the United States produced 10,000 bales of cotton. Fifty years later it produced 1.5 million bales. At that time, American cotton accounted for 60 percent of the world's cotton and two-thirds of American exports.

Life in the South

The owners of cotton plantations were called planters. They grew rich from the sale of cotton. They built large plantation homes on their estates where they lived with their families. Wealthy planters also built magnificent buildings and churches in southern cities such as Savannah in Georgia, Natchez and New Orleans in Louisiana, and Charleston in South Carolina. Most of the people who lived in the South were slaves who worked in the fields. Some slaves also worked in planters' homes, cooking, cleaning, and looking after planters' children.

American Civil War

By the mid-1800s, the South was running out of new land for growing cotton, so southern planters looked to the West for more cotton lands. In the northern states, members of a growing movement called the Abolition movement did not want slave states to exist. In the northern states, the economy was based on industry, which did not rely directly on slave labor. Beginning in 1861, the North and South fought one another in a bloody civil war. One of the main issues of the war was slavery. Southern plantation owners and other white Southerners felt they had a right to own slaves while in the North, abolitionists argued that the slaves should be set free. In 1865 the South lost the American Civil War and the slaves were freed.

Poverty and hunger were a reality for many in the South after the war.

Slavery

Slavery began in the United States in 1619, when twenty slaves were brought to the Jamestown colony. Two hundred years later, the demand for raw cotton and the invention of the cotton gin expanded slavery in the American South. For cotton cultivation to be profitable, a large and cheap labor force was needed. At the same time, buying and keeping slaves cost planters a lot of money, which cotton provided.

The history of cotton growing and production is also a history of slavery.

Slave Ports

Savannah, Georgia, was an important port city in the South. It was a center for trade where cash crops were sold and exported. It was also an entry port for slaves coming into the United States. The slave trade brought millions of black slaves to Savannah. By 1860, there were almost four million slaves in the United States. In the South, 37 percent of the population was black, and almost all of them were slaves. Slaves worked in the fields on cotton and rice plantations, as skilled workers and as servants in the homes of planters.

BALING COTTON.

GINNING COTTON

In the Fields

Field slaves on cotton plantations worked under the gang system. In the gang system, slaves were divided into crews, or small groups. Crews worked together in a part of the cotton field under the watchful eye of a white **overseer**. On larger plantations, drivers watched over the work of slaves in the fields. The overseer or driver was supposed to make sure that slaves were working hard all day. They punished slaves who they felt were not working hard enough by whipping them and threatening to separate them from their families by selling them to faraway plantations. Slaves in cotton fields worked from dawn to dusk, 12 to 16 hours a day year-round. Their only break was the fourth of July and a week at Christmas.

Property and Rights

Slaves were considered the property of their owners. Plantation owners often **branded** slaves on the chest or face with a hot iron so they were easily identified if they tried to run away. Slave patrols watched the roads for unknown slaves. Slaves had to carry passes signed by their owners allowing them to leave the plantation. Under some southern laws, it was illegal for slave owners to teach slaves to read or write. Laws also made it illegal for owners to abuse or kill their slaves, but because slaves could not testify in court, few plantation owners were found guilty of these crimes. Some slaves were allowed to buy their freedom with money they made working other jobs after their plantation work was finished. Others who wanted their freedom ran away. Slaves who remained on the plantation resisted their situation by destroying crops and tools, working at a slow pace, or pretending to be ill to escape work.

A Slave's Life

Most slaves lived in dirt-floor shacks on the plantation. Their living conditions were cramped and entire families lived in one room. In the South, slave marriages were not legally recognized. Slave women were encouraged to have many children, because their children were born slaves. Some women were rewarded with a silver coin or a bolt of cloth by their plantation owners for having children. Women worked among the men in the fields during the day and had to care for their children, cook, and sew clothing for their families at night. The main meal for southern slaves was corn and pork, and some slaves also hunted possum.

A photo of a slave's back shows the scarring left from repeated whippings.

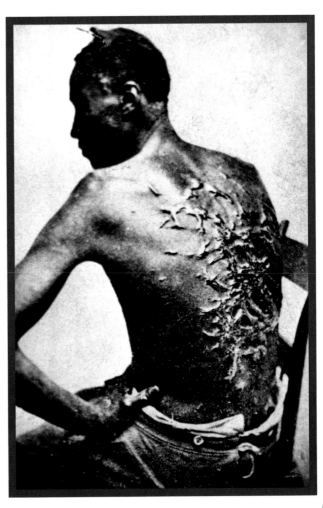

Mill Towns

In the early 1800s, the northern states began to **industrialize**. Textile factories, or mills, were built to make cotton cloth. Early mills specialized in one part of textile manufacturing. Raw cotton was spun at one mill, then shipped to another mill to be made into cloth. In later factories, raw cotton was made into finished cloth in one place.

Lowell's Mill

In 1810, Francis Cabot Lowell, son of a wealthy Boston merchant family, toured the textile mills of Manchester, England. Manchester was a city blackened by pollution from coal burned to power factory machines. Orphaned children as young as eight years old worked in mills.

Child Workers

Child workers were beaten by their supervisors and made to sleep six to a room. Lowell was impressed by the machinery he saw in the mills, but repulsed by the way workers lived. He memorized the way the machines worked in Manchester factories. Back in the United States, Lowell used his family's ties with other wealthy New England families to raise money to build a factory on the Charles River in Waltham, Massachusetts. In 1814, the textile mill opened, which used America's first power loom for weaving cloth. Lowell called his new business the Boston Manufacturing Company. By 1815, more than 27 million pounds of cotton were being shipped to the North from the South.

24

Lords of the Loom

Lowell's mill was moved to the Merrimack River, outside of Boston, after his death in 1817. Here, the first American city built around making textiles was established. It was called Lowell. By 1837, Lowell had a population of 18,000 people, 6,000 of which worked in the mills. Company houses and stores were built for workers to live in and shop at. Everything in the mill town revolved around the mill.

Life of a Mill Worker

Whole families, including children as young as eight years old, worked in some textile mills. In Lowell, the factory workers were almost all women and their supervisors were almost always men. Factory work allowed young, unmarried women to have an income. Women did the jobs of spinning and weaving. Bells rang to start work, signal breaks, and end the work day.

Factory windows were often nailed shut to keep the humidity, or air moisture, in. This helped to prevent threads from breaking. Poor air circulation made many mill workers sick from breathing in fibers all day. Mill workers often went to work ill because they were not paid for sick days off and had to pay to use the mill's infirmary, or hospital. After work, mill workers who were not too tired, met with friends, read books, or listened to guest speakers at a local meeting hall. The women workers lived in boarding houses close to the mill. The lives of the women were strictly watched by housemothers, who made sure that they had little contact with men and attended church on Sundays.

(above) Many mill jobs were dangerous. Some mills used children, who climbed under machines to collect bits of cotton. Workers often lost fingers in machines.

Worker Reforms

Young women came from farms to start work in the mills between the ages of 16 and 21. Most factory women worked in the mills for about three years. Around the 1840s, mill owners tried to cut mill workers' wages. The workers banded together to push for reform, such as shorter work days and better working conditions. In response, mill owners in the North began to hire **immigrant** French Canadian and Irish workers. Immigrant workers were paid less money to do the same work as other workers. Tensions rose among the workers and between the workers and the mill owners. In Philadelphia, factory workers went on **strike** and rioted in the 1840s.

Southern Mills

In the 1880s, smaller textile mills from the North began to move to the South. Mill towns in the South were based around rural villages. Mill agents and superintendents controlled the towns. The mill company provided jobs, houses, food, and clothing for all the workers. At first, mill workers were hard to find in the South. Newly freed slaves worked in some mills, but they were used to working in fields and many did not like factory work. White workers often refused to work with black workers.

(above) Striking textile workers in Atlanta held up a train engine and railroad cars near the Exposition Cotton Mills in the 1930s. Police exploded a tear gas bomb in their midst.

▲ *The Lowell Offering magazine written and published by women working at Lowell mills.*

Striking Mill Workers

In the 1880s and 1890s, the Knights of Labor and the National Union of Textile Workers organized southern mill workers into unions. Unions represented the rights of the workers. Major strikes happened in 1912 and 1913 in northern mills. By the 1920s, northern mills had to compete with new synthetic, or human-made, textiles and cheap cloth imported from Japan. More northern mills moved south and others closed. In southern mills, workers were upset by having to manage more machines, work night shifts, and take pay cuts. In 1934, the National Union of Textile Workers called for a general strike and nearly 500,000 workers in 21 states walked off the job. Most striking workers lost their jobs because mill owners would not hire them back after the strike ended.

The Boll Weevil

The boll weevil did not destroy the cotton crops of the entire South. In some regions such as the Mississippi delta, the crop was unharmed. Georgia, Alabama, North Carolina, and South Carolina were hit the hardest by infestations.

Growing one main cash crop, such as the South did with cotton, is called monoculture. The danger with monoculture is that if something happens to destroy or threaten the crop, then the economy based around that crop suffers as well. In 1892, the boll weevil, an insect that attacks cotton plants, migrated from Central America and reached Texas. The boll weevil uses its long snout to bore into cotton pods and suck out the cotton fibers. The female boll weevil also uses her snout to drill holes in cotton bolls and flower buds for depositing her eggs. She lays from 100 to 300 eggs. The larvae, or young boll weevils, eat all the fibers inside the boll before growing into adults.

Decimated Crops and Depression

Boll weevil infestations wiped out cotton crops. By 1922, the boll weevil had spread to almost all cotton-growing areas of the United States. With crops destroyed, farmers lost their farms and their homes, and banks and towns went bankrupt.

After the American Civil War, large cotton plantations were broken up into smaller farms. The land was leased, or rented, to black and white farmers to work. This system of farming was called sharecropping. Boll weevil infestations destroyed the farmers' and sharecroppers' crops, which left them on the brink of starvation. The desperate economic state of the South was made worse during the **Great Depression** of the 1930s.

Away from Cotton

Many southern farmers gave up on growing cotton after the boll weevil arrived. They began to plant other cash crops, such as corn, soybeans, and peanuts. Other farmers moved further West, to areas where the boll weevil had not yet spread, such as California, and planted large cotton fields there. Other people gave up on farming altogether and went to work in the textile mills.

▸ *Pheromone traps attract female boll weevils and trap them before they can attack cotton plants.*

(below) During the Great Depression many cotton farming families left their land because of boll weevil infestations and drought. Poor and near-starving, they traveled west to find new jobs.

Miracle Science

As early as 1903, the Texas Legislature offered a cash reward to anyone who could find a way to control the boll weevil problem. From 1914 until the 1940s, farmers were urged to dust, or spray, their cotton with a chemical called calcium arsenate, or arsenic. In the late 1940s, chemical companies in North America began to sell a chemical called DDT to cotton farmers to protect their cotton crops from boll weevils. DDT and other pesticides are toxic to the environment. They poison fish and animals. Boll weevils survived all chemical attempts to kill them by building up a **natural resistance**. It was not until 1966 that scientists found a safe way to control boll weevils. Laboratory studies showed that male boll weevils produced a pheromone, or natural chemical that attracted females. From the studies, pheromone traps were developed.

World Cotton Today

Sweatshops produce cotton clothing and textiles cheaply by not paying their workers fair wages. Consumers can protest against sweatshops by refusing to buy goods made this way.

For some countries around the world, such as those in Central and West Africa, cotton is the country's main export. If their cotton crops fail, or if there is a drought in the region, small-scale farmers risk starvation. In the United States, cotton farmers receive money from the federal government, called subsidies, to grow cotton. The cost of growing cotton is higher in the United States than in African countries because American farmers depend on expensive planting and harvesting machines. In Africa and India, cotton is harvested by hand.

From Farm to Market

In the United States today, cotton farmers sell their cotton to a ginnery to remove the seeds. The cotton fibers are then sold to a cotton merchant. The merchant then sells the cotton to mills or to other merchants in foreign countries at a commodities exchange, or a place where goods that are in demand are bought and sold. Several factors can hurt the price of cotton on the world market, such as there being too much cotton to sell. Other factors cause prices to rise, such as when bad weather ruins crops.

Protecting the Crop

To protect cotton crops from pests without spraying chemicals, scientists have developed genetically modified cotton plants. Genetic modification is the process in which scientists change a plant's natural structure to make it perform in different ways. For example, genetically modified cotton plants grown in India produce a higher **yield**. Some people argue that genetically modified cotton will wipe out other types of cotton.

Cotton Workers

In countries where cotton farmers cannot afford farm machinery, workers are paid to do the work by hand. In order to make as much profit as possible from the sale of cotton, some farmers keep workers' wages low.

In India and Uzbekistan, organizations that study child labor have reported that children are used to work in cotton fields. In some cases, farmers loan money to parents if they allow their children to work. In others cases, children are paid just pennies a day or not at all.

Sweatshops

Sweatshops are factories where workers are paid very little to make clothing and other goods from textiles. In sweatshops, worker safety is often ignored and workers are not paid benefits. Since the 1980s, reports have shown that sweatshops employ mostly young women, much like the textile mills of the past. Using sweatshops allows big clothing manufacturers to make more profit from the sale of their goods.

In many areas of the world, cotton is still grown and harvested by hand. Organic cotton, or natural cotton, is grown without using pesticides.

Glossary

Arab A person from the Middle East or North Africa who speaks the Arabic language

archaeologists A person who studies ancient buildings and cultures

boom A period of great interest or sales

brand To mark a person's flesh to show that they are the property of someone else

cash crop A crop grown primarily to sell, and designed to make the grower money

compensation Money given to make up for money previously earned but not received

crossbreed When two varieties of plant come together to make a new type of plant

crown Members of royalty that rule a country

drawn to pull

empire A group of countries under one ruler

Great Depression A period during the 1930s of drought and economic hardship

Hindu A person who follows Hinduism, a religion originating in India

humidity The amount of moisture in the air

immigrant A person who moves to another country

Industrial Revolution A period starting in the late 1700s in England, when people began moving to cities to work in factories

industrialize The act of creating more factories, so more goods can be produced

irrigate To water using human-made devices

natural resistance A plant or animal's ability to fight and survive disease or chemicals that usually kill

New World The name given to North, Central, and South America by Europeans

nutrients Substances that help living things grow

overseer Managers or supervisors in charge of other workers

pressed To flatten or put pressure on something so more units can be packed together

processed A good that is manufactured or changed from its original state

quality Something that has value

shuttle The part on a loom that carries the weft thread.

strike To refuse to work as a way of protesting

yield The amount of crop produced in a season

Index

1 2 3 4 5 6 7 8 9 0 Printed in the U.S.A. 4 3 2 1 0 9 8 7 6 5